The Biodiverse Garden Month by Month

A Practical Guide to Creating a
Wildlife Haven in Your
Own Backyard

By

RK Wardell

Copyright © 2024 RK Wardell All rights reserved.
ISBN: 9798343565690
Independently published by RK Wardell. No part of this publication may be reproduced, distributed, or transmitted in any form or by any means, including photocopying, recording, or other electronic or mechanical methods, without the prior written permission of the publisher, except in the case of brief quotations embodied in critical reviews and certain other non-commercial uses permitted by copyright law.

Dedication

I want to express my deepest gratitude to the extraordinary women who have nurtured my love for the natural world and inspired me to cultivate a life of growth and abundance:
To Gilly, my beloved partner, whose unwavering support and shared passion for gardening have blossomed into a shared sanctuary of love and beauty. Thank you for being my constant companion, my fellow adventurer, and my inspiration.

To Helen and Gill, my cherished sisters, whose unwavering belief in me has been a constant source of strength and encouragement. Thank you for always being there to lend a helping hand, both in the garden and in life.

About the Author

RK Wardell is a retired IT project manager with a lifelong passion for gardening and a deep appreciation for the interconnectedness of all living things. His interest in entrepreneurship and self-help has led him to explore the many ways in which personal growth and development can be nurtured through a connection with the natural world.

A lifelong Liverpool Football Club fan, he finds solace and inspiration in the rhythms of nature and the camaraderie of the garden. He currently resides in leafy Surrey, England, where he tends to his own garden, a haven for wildlife and a source of endless fascination and joy.

Table of Contents

1. Welcome to the Biodiversity Garden (January)
2. Early Spring Awakening (February)
3. Buzzing with Life (March)
4. A Symphony of Colours (April)
5. Abundant Blooms (May)
6. Summer Harvest (June)
7. Peak Season (July)
8. Late Summer Bounty (August)
9. Autumn Abundance (September)
10. Preparing for Winter (October)
11. Winter Rest (November)
12. A Time for Renewal (December)

Chapter 1: Welcome to the Biodiversity Garden (January)

The crisp winter air bites at my cheeks as I step into the garden. Frost sparkles on the dormant grass, and the skeletal branches of the old oak tree reach towards the steely grey sky. It may seem like a time of slumber, but beneath the surface, life is stirring. This is where our journey begins, in the quiet anticipation of January, as we embark on creating a garden that not only thrives but teems with the vibrant symphony of biodiversity.

For years, I've been fascinated by the intricate web of life that exists within a garden. It's a microcosm of our planet, a place where plants, animals, fungi, and microorganisms intertwine in a delicate dance of interdependence. As a gardener and author, I've witnessed firsthand the magic that unfolds when we invite nature to take centre stage.

Biodiversity, simply put, is the variety of life. It's the buzzing of bees, the fluttering of butterflies, the rustling of hedgehogs in the undergrowth. It's the rich tapestry of plants, from the towering sunflowers to the humble earthworms beneath our feet. And it's crucial, not just for the health of our planet, but for the resilience and productivity of our gardens.

Imagine your garden as a bustling city, a vibrant hub where plants, insects, and creatures of all kinds live and interact. When we embrace biodiversity, we're essentially creating a thriving metropolis, a place of incredible interconnectedness and resilience.

By cultivating a rich tapestry of life in our gardens, we're not just creating a feast for the eyes. We're building a robust and adaptable ecosystem, one that can weather storms both literal and metaphorical—from unexpected pests to the shifting tides of our climate.

But the benefits of biodiversity extend far beyond the practical. There's a certain magic, an almost primal joy, in witnessing the symphony of life unfold in a garden you've helped to create. It's a feeling of deep connection to the natural world, a sense of purpose that transcends the simple act of gardening.

Planning Your Biodiversity Garden
Before we grab our trowels and seeds, let's take a moment to plan our biodiversity haven. Every garden is unique, and understanding your space is the first step.

- Assess your space and resources: Take a walk around your garden. Observe the sunlight patterns, soil conditions, and existing plants. How much space do you have? What are your limitations? Are there any microclimates – shady corners, sunny spots, or damp areas? Make a note of any existing features like trees, fences, or walls that can be incorporated into your design. Consider your resources too: How much time can you dedicate to gardening? What is your budget? Honest answers here will help you create a garden you can realistically manage and enjoy.

- Choosing the right plants: Native plants are the cornerstone of a biodiverse garden. They have co-evolved with local wildlife, providing the ideal food and habitat. Research the native plants in your region and select a variety that will attract pollinators, birds, and other beneficial creatures. Think beyond flowers! Include a diverse mix of flowering plants, trees, shrubs, and groundcovers to create a multi-layered habitat that caters to a wide range of creatures. For example, berry-producing shrubs provide food for birds, while dense evergreen shrubs offer shelter and nesting sites.

- Designing for wildlife: Think like a creature seeking shelter and sustenance. Create a variety of habitats within your garden. Plant dense shrubs for nesting birds, leave a patch of wildflowers for pollinators, and consider adding a water feature like a birdbath or small pond. Incorporate elements that provide shelter, such as piles of leaves, logs, or rocks. Vary the height and density of your plantings to create different niches for different species. Remember, even a small balcony can become a haven for biodiversity with the right plants and a little creativity. Vertical gardens, hanging baskets, and container plantings can all contribute to a thriving ecosystem.

January Gardening Tasks

Even in the depths of winter, there's plenty to do to prepare for the season ahead.

- Soil testing and improvement: Healthy soil is the foundation of a thriving garden. Now is the perfect time to test your soil's pH and nutrient levels. You can purchase a home soil testing kit or send a sample to a professional lab for analysis. Based on the results, amend the soil with compost, well-rotted manure, or other organic matter to improve its structure and fertility. Adding organic matter improves drainage in clay soils and water retention in sandy soils, creating a more hospitable environment for plant roots.

- Planning your seed starting schedule: Grab a cup of tea and your favourite gardening catalogues. Decide which plants you want to grow from seed and create a seed starting schedule based on their germination times and your last frost date. Consider staggering your plantings to ensure a continuous harvest throughout the season. For example, you could sow a few lettuce seeds every couple of weeks to enjoy fresh salads for a longer period.

- Ordering seeds and supplies: Don't wait until spring to order your seeds and gardening supplies. Many seed companies have limited stock, so order early to ensure you get the varieties you want. This is also a good time to stock up on essential tools like trowels, hand rakes, and pruning shears.
- Winter pruning: Fruit trees and shrubs often benefit from winter pruning while they are dormant. Remove any dead, damaged, or crossing branches to encourage healthy growth and shape the plant. This is also a good time to remove any diseased or pest-infested branches to prevent problems in the coming season. Be sure to use sharp, clean pruning tools to avoid damaging the plant.

Featured Plant: Winter Aconite (Eranthis hyemalis)

One of my favourite early bloomers is the Winter Aconite. These cheerful yellow flowers emerge even when snow is still on the ground, providing a vital source of nectar for early pollinators like bees and hoverflies. Their cup-shaped blossoms resemble miniature buttercups, bringing a welcome splash of colour to the winter garden. Plant them in well-drained soil in a sunny or partially shaded spot, and they'll naturalise readily, forming a charming carpet of gold. They combine beautifully with other early spring bulbs like snowdrops and crocuses. Interestingly, Winter Aconite is a member of the buttercup family and contains cardiac glycosides, which make it mildly toxic to humans and animals if ingested. This is a good reminder that even in a biodiverse garden, it's important to be aware of the properties of the plants we grow.

DIY Project: Building a Bird Feeder

Inviting birds into your garden is a wonderful way to enhance biodiversity. This month let's build a simple bird feeder to provide them with much-needed sustenance during the colder months.

Materials:
- Clean, empty plastic bottle (any size)
- Scissors
- String or twine
- Wooden dowel or twig (for perches, optional)
- Bird seed

Instructions:
1. **Prepare the bottle:** Remove any labels and wash the bottle thoroughly. Let it dry completely.
2. **Create feeding holes:** Carefully cut two small holes on opposite sides of the bottle, about 2-3 inches from the bottom. These holes should be large enough for birds to access the seed but not so large that the seed spills out easily.
3. **Add perches (optional):** If you want to provide perches for the birds, poke two small holes opposite each other just above each feeding hole. Slide the dowel or twig through the holes to create perches.
4. **Create drainage holes:** Poke a few small holes in the bottom of the bottle to allow for drainage in case of rain.
5. **Make a hanging loop:** Near the top of the bottle, poke two holes opposite each other. Thread the string or twine through the holes and tie a knot to create a loop for hanging.
6. **Fill with seed:** Fill the bottle with bird seed. You can use a funnel to make this easier.
7. **Hang your feeder:** Hang the feeder from a tree branch, hook, or any other suitable location. Choose a spot that is sheltered from strong winds and rain, and where you can easily observe the birds that visit.

Tips:
- **Smooth the edges:** Smooth any rough edges around the holes with sandpaper or a nail file to prevent birds from injuring themselves.
- **Decorate your feeder:** Get creative and decorate the bottle with paint, markers, or other materials.
- **Choose the right seed:** Different birds prefer different types of seed. A mix of sunflower seeds, millet, and nyjer seed will attract a variety of birds.
- **Keep it clean:** Clean the feeder regularly with warm soapy water to prevent the spread of diseases.

This simple bird feeder is a great way to recycle a plastic bottle and provide food for your feathered friends. It's a fun and easy project that can be enjoyed by people of all ages.

Garden Journal Prompt:
Take a walk around your garden and observe the signs of life that are present even in winter. Do you see any birds, insects, or other creatures? What plants are still green or showing signs of new growth? Record your observations in your journal and reflect on the ways you can enhance your garden's biodiversity in the coming year.

As we close this first chapter, I invite you to step into your garden, breathe in the fresh air, and embrace the potential that lies dormant within the winter landscape. Together, let's embark on this journey of creating a garden that not only nourishes us but also provides a sanctuary for the incredible diversity of life that surrounds us.

Chapter 2: Early Spring Awakening (February)

A palpable shift occurs in February. The days lengthen, and the sun's rays gain strength. A sense of anticipation hangs in the air, a promise of renewal and rebirth. In the garden, the first brave shoots emerge from the cold earth, and the symphony of life begins to crescendo. This is a time of awakening, a time to nurture the burgeoning biodiversity that will shape our garden's destiny.

Creating Habitats for Beneficial Insects

As the garden stirs to life, so do the beneficial insects that play a vital role in its health and productivity. These tiny creatures are our allies, pollinating our flowers, controlling pests, and enriching the soil. To welcome them into our gardens, we must provide them with the food and shelter they need to thrive.

- Importance of providing shelter: Overwintering insects need safe havens to survive the cold months. Leaf litter, hollow stems, and clumps of grasses provide vital refuge. Resist the urge to tidy up too meticulously in autumn, leaving some areas undisturbed to offer shelter for these beneficial creatures. Different insects have different preferences. Ladybugs like to snuggle into dry leaves and crevices, while lacewings seek out the shelter of evergreen shrubs. Ground beetles, important predators of slugs and snails, seek refuge under logs and stones. By providing a variety of habitats, we can cater to the needs of a diverse range of beneficial insects. Think about creating a "bug hotel" in a quiet corner of your garden. This can be as simple as a pile of logs and branches, or a more elaborate structure made from recycled materials like pallets, bricks, and tiles.

- Building insect hotels and bug boxes: Supplement natural shelters with purpose-built insect hotels. These structures provide nesting sites and overwintering habitats for a variety of beneficial insects, including solitary bees, ladybugs, and lacewings. You can easily create your own insect hotel using natural materials like bamboo canes, pinecones, and straw. Drill holes of varying sizes (between 2mm and 10mm in diameter) into logs or blocks of wood to provide nesting sites for different species. Include a variety of materials to create different microhabitats within the hotel. For example, ladybugs prefer tight spaces, so include some sections with tightly packed straw or dried leaves. Lacewings, on the other hand, prefer more open spaces, so include some sections with larger cavities. Place your insect hotel in a sunny, sheltered location, preferably near flowering plants.

- Planting early blooming flowers: Early-blooming flowers provide a vital source of nectar and pollen for pollinators emerging from their winter slumber. Crocuses, snowdrops, and winter aconites are excellent choices, offering a welcome feast for hungry bees and butterflies. Consider planting a succession of early bloomers to provide a continuous source of food for pollinators throughout the early spring. *Hellebores,* with their nodding, cup-shaped flowers, are a particularly good choice, as they bloom for a long period and provide shelter for insects as well as food. Lungwort (*Pulmonaria*) is another excellent early bloomer, with its attractive spotted leaves and clusters of pink, purple, or blue flowers.

February Gardening Tasks

February is a time of preparation, a time to sow the seeds of a bountiful and biodiverse garden.

- Starting seeds indoors: Many plants benefit from an early start indoors, giving them a head start on the growing season. Prepare your seed trays, pots, and growing medium. Use a sterile seed-starting mix to prevent damping-off disease, a fungal infection that can kill seedlings. Sow seeds according to their individual requirements, paying attention to depth and spacing. For example, tiny seeds like lettuce should be sown shallowly, while larger seeds like beans can be sown deeper. Provide adequate light, warmth, and moisture for germination. A sunny windowsill is often sufficient, but you may need to supplement with grow lights if your home is particularly dark. Keep the growing medium moist but not waterlogged and ensure good air circulation to prevent fungal diseases. Remember to label your seedlings clearly with the plant name and sowing date! Some seeds, like tomatoes and peppers, require warm temperatures to germinate (around 20-25°C), while others, like lettuce and spinach, can germinate in cooler conditions (around 10-15°C).

- Preparing garden beds: As the ground thaws, it's time to prepare your garden beds for planting. Begin by removing any weeds that have emerged over the winter. Then, loosen the soil with a garden fork to improve drainage and aeration. Add compost or other organic matter to improve its fertility and structure. If you have heavy clay soil, consider double digging to improve drainage. This involves digging a trench and turning the soil over to a depth of two spades. If your soil is sandy, add plenty of organic matter to improve water retention. You can also use this time to create raised beds or improve existing ones. Raised beds offer several advantages, including improved drainage, warmer soil temperatures, and easier access for gardening.

- Protecting early seedlings: Early seedlings are vulnerable to frost, which can damage or kill them. Protect them with cloches, row covers, or cold frames until the danger of frost has passed. Cloches are individual covers that protect individual plants or small groups of plants. Row covers are long sheets of fabric that can be draped over entire rows of plants. Cold frames are miniature greenhouses that provide a more controlled environment for seedlings. Harden off seedlings gradually by exposing them to outdoor conditions for increasing periods each day before planting them out. This helps them acclimate to the harsher conditions of the garden, such as wind, sun, and temperature fluctuations.

Featured Plant: Crocus (Crocus spp.)
Crocuses are a quintessential symbol of spring, their vibrant blooms pushing through the earth with an irrepressible zest for life. These cheerful flowers are not only a delight to behold but also a valuable source of early-season nectar for bees and other pollinators. Plant them in well-drained soil in a sunny location, and they will reward you with a vibrant display of colour year after year.

There are many different species and cultivars of crocus, offering a wide range of colours and bloom times. Some, like *Crocus tommasinianus*, naturalise readily, creating a carpet of purple blooms. Others, like *Crocus chrysanthus*, offer a variety of colours, including yellow, white, and blue. Crocuses are also relatively low-maintenance and deer-resistant, making them an excellent choice for a biodiversity garden. They are particularly attractive to bumblebees, which are important pollinators of many fruit and vegetable crops. In folklore, crocuses are associated with new beginnings and hope, making them a fitting symbol for the awakening of spring.

DIY Project: Making Seed Bombs
Seed bombs are a delightful way to introduce wildflowers into your garden or neglected areas in your neighbourhood. They are simply a mixture of clay, compost, and wildflower seeds that can be tossed into areas where you want to encourage wildflowers to grow.

Materials:
- **Clay:** Air-dry clay or powdered clay (found in craft stores) is ideal. You can also use clay soil if you have it in your garden.
- **Compost:** Use peat-free compost for a more sustainable option.
- **Wildflower seeds:** Choose a mix of wildflower seeds that are suitable for your region and growing conditions. (More on this below!)
- **Water:** For binding the ingredients.
- **Mixing bowl:** For combining the ingredients.

Instructions:
1. **Combine the dry ingredients:** In a mixing bowl, combine 1 cup of wildflower seeds with 5 cups of compost and 2-3 cups of clay powder (or clay soil).
2. **Add water gradually:** Slowly add water to the mixture, mixing with your hands until everything sticks together. The consistency should be like a thick dough, firm enough to hold its shape but not too wet.
3. **Roll into balls:** Roll the mixture into firm balls, about the size of a golf ball.
4. **Dry the seed bombs:** Leave the seed bombs to dry in a sunny spot for a day or two, or until they are completely dry and hardened.
5. **Launch your seed bombs!** Toss or gently throw your seed bombs into bare patches of ground where you want wildflowers to grow. You can also tuck them into crevices in walls or pavements.

Choosing the Right Wildflower Seed Mix:
The success of your seed bombs depends on choosing the right wildflower seed mix. Here are some factors to consider:

- **Your region:** Select a mix that is appropriate for your climate and growing conditions.
- **Soil type:** Choose seeds that are suited to your soil type, whether it's clay, sandy, or loamy.
- **Sunlight:** Consider the amount of sunlight the area receives. Some wildflowers thrive in full sun, while others prefer shade.
- **Purpose:** Do you want to attract pollinators, create a wildflower meadow, or simply add a splash of colour to a neglected area? Choose a seed mix that aligns with your goals.

Here are some examples of suitable wildflower seed mixes:
- **Pollinator mix:** This mix might include seeds for flowers like cornflowers, poppies, and cosmos, which are attractive to bees, butterflies, and other pollinators.
- **Meadow mix:** This mix might include a variety of grasses and wildflowers, such as oxeye daisies, yellow rattle, and red clover, to create a mini meadow.
- **Native wildflower mix:** This mix focuses on wildflowers that are native to your region, providing the ideal food and habitat for local wildlife.

Tips for Seed Bomb Success:
- **Don't overwater:** Seed bombs need some moisture to germinate, but too much water can cause them to rot. Rely on rainfall or water sparingly.
- **Choose the right location:** Toss your seed bombs in areas that receive adequate sunlight and have suitable soil conditions.
- **Be patient:** Wildflowers can take time to germinate and grow. Don't be discouraged if you don't see results immediately.
- **Have fun!** Seed bombing is a fun and creative way to spread wildflowers and enhance biodiversity.
-

Enjoy the process of creating and launching your seed bombs and watch as they transform bare patches of ground into vibrant displays of wildflowers.

Did You Know?
Some solitary bees can pollinate up to 300 flowers per day, making them incredibly efficient pollinators! By providing nesting sites for these bees in your garden, you can significantly increase the pollination of your fruits, vegetables, and flowers.

Garden Journal Prompt:
As you observe the first signs of spring in your garden, take a moment to reflect on the interconnectedness of life. How do the plants, insects, and other creatures in your garden depend on each other? What role can you play in fostering this web of life? Record your thoughts and observations in your journal.

The awakening of spring brings a sense of hope and renewal. By embracing the principles of biodiversity, we can create a garden that is not only beautiful but also a thriving ecosystem, teeming with life and contributing to the health of our planet.

Chapter 3: Buzzing with Life (March)

March arrives with a palpable sense of urgency. The soil thaws, buds swell, and the first pollinators emerge, blinking in the strengthening sunlight. It's a month of vibrant activity, a time to harness the burgeoning energy of spring and create a garden that hums with life. As the garden awakens, we must shift our attention from the structural elements and soil preparation that dominated the winter months to the vibrant world of pollinators and the plants that sustain them.

Attracting Pollinators

Pollinators are the lifeblood of a healthy garden, ensuring the reproduction of countless plants, including many of our favourite fruits and vegetables. As gardeners, we have a responsibility to support these vital creatures by creating a welcoming habitat that caters to their needs. A garden teeming with pollinators is not only a joy to behold but also a vital contributor to the health of the wider ecosystem.

While honeybees often steal the limelight, a diverse range of pollinators contributes to the health of our gardens. Bumblebees, with their furry bodies and long tongues, are particularly adept at pollinating deep-throated flowers like foxgloves and comfrey. Their size and strength allow them to 'buzz pollinate', shaking pollen loose from flowers like tomatoes and blueberries. Solitary bees, such as mason bees and leafcutter bees, are incredibly efficient pollinators, often visiting far more flowers per day than honeybees. They are also less likely to sting, making them ideal garden companions.

Hoverflies, with their delicate wings and hovering flight, are also important pollinators, particularly of shallow flowers like daisies and umbellifers. Their larvae are voracious predators of aphids, making them doubly beneficial in the garden. Butterflies and moths, with their long proboscises, are drawn to fragrant, nectar-rich blooms like buddleias and honeysuckle. By understanding the preferences of different pollinators, we can choose a diverse range of plants that cater to their needs.

A key principle of attracting pollinators is to provide a continuous source of nectar and pollen throughout the growing season. This means choosing a variety of plants that flower at different times, from early spring to late autumn. Include a mix of shapes, sizes, and colours to attract a wide range of pollinators. Single flowers, with their open structures and accessible nectar, are generally preferred by pollinators over double flowers, which often have reduced nectar and pollen due to their dense petal formations.

Native wildflowers are particularly valuable, as they have co-evolved with local pollinators and provide the ideal food source. In my own garden, I've found that a combination of early-flowering bulbs like crocuses and snowdrops, followed by hardy annuals like calendula and cosmos, and then later-flowering perennials like asters and sedums, provides a continuous source of nectar and pollen for pollinators throughout the season.

Pollinators need water for drinking and cooling, especially during hot weather. A shallow dish filled with water and pebbles provides a safe landing spot for bees and butterflies. The pebbles give them something to grip onto and prevent them from drowning.

You can also create a bog garden or install a small pond to provide a more permanent water source. Include a variety of water depths and emergent plants to cater to different species. Ensure that the water is clean and refreshed regularly to prevent mosquito breeding. In drier climates, consider installing a small water feature with a gentle trickle or drip, as the sound of moving water can attract pollinators from afar.

March Gardening Tasks
March is a month of action, a time to put our gardening plans into practice and nurture the emerging life in our gardens. The increasing daylight hours and warmer temperatures trigger a burst of growth, and we must be ready to respond to the needs of our plants.

If you've started seeds indoors, it's time to harden off your seedlings before planting them out. This involves gradually acclimating them to outdoor conditions by exposing them to increasing periods of sunlight, wind, and temperature fluctuations. Start by placing them in a sheltered spot for a few hours each day, gradually increasing the exposure time over a week or two. This process helps them develop stronger stems and leaves and reduces the shock of transplanting. If you experience a cold snap, be sure to bring your seedlings back indoors or protect them with cloches or fleece.

Many hardy vegetables, such as peas, broad beans, spinach, and radishes, can be sown directly into the ground in March. Prepare the soil by removing weeds and adding compost. Sow seeds according to the packet instructions, paying attention to depth and spacing. Water gently and keep the soil moist until the seedlings emerge.

To prevent birds from eating your seeds, cover the area with netting or fleece until the seedlings are a few inches tall. You can also use this time to sow hardy annual flowers, such as calendula, cornflowers, and poppies, directly into the ground.

Early spring crops, such as onions, shallots, and potatoes, can also be planted in March. Choose a sunny location with well-drained soil. Plant onions and shallots at the correct depth, ensuring that the tips are just below the soil surface. Plant potatoes in trenches or raised beds, spacing them according to the variety. If you're short on space, consider growing potatoes in containers or bags.

Featured Plant: Borage (Borago officinalis)
Borage is a delightful herb with vibrant blue, star-shaped flowers that are a magnet for bees. It's a valuable addition to any biodiversity garden, providing a rich source of nectar and pollen for a wide range of pollinators. Borage is also a versatile culinary herb, with its cucumber-flavoured leaves and edible flowers adding a unique touch to salads, soups, and drinks. The plant is easy to grow, thriving in full sun and well-drained soil. It readily self-seeds, ensuring a continuous supply of this bee-friendly herb in your garden. Borage is also known for its medicinal properties, traditionally used to treat a variety of ailments, including fever, coughs, and skin conditions.

Recipe: Borage Blossom Salad
This simple salad showcases the delicate flavour of borage blossoms.

Ingredients:
- 1 cup borage blossoms
- 1 cup mixed salad greens
- 1/4 cup chopped cucumber
- 1/4 cup chopped red onion
- 2 tablespoons olive oil
- 1 tablespoon lemon juice
- Salt and pepper to taste

Instructions:
1. Gently wash the borage blossoms and salad greens.
2. Combine the borage blossoms, salad greens, cucumber, and red onion in a bowl.
3. Whisk together the olive oil and lemon juice in a separate bowl.
4. Pour the dressing over the salad and toss gently.
5. Season with salt and pepper to taste.

Garden Journal Prompt:
Observe the pollinators visiting your garden this month. Which flowers are most attractive to them? What other steps can you take to support these vital creatures? Record your observations and ideas in your journal.

March is a month of vibrant activity and growth, a time to celebrate the interconnectedness of life in our gardens. By creating a welcoming habitat for pollinators, we can ensure the health and productivity of our gardens while contributing to the wider ecosystem.

Chapter 4: A Symphony of Colours (April)

April unfolds like a vibrant tapestry, a symphony of colours and textures as the garden bursts into life. It's a month of rapid growth and abundant blooms, a time to celebrate the beauty of nature's artistry and harness its power to create a resilient and harmonious ecosystem. As we move further into spring, our focus shifts to nurturing the burgeoning life in our gardens and fostering the intricate relationships between plants and their environment. This is the time to truly appreciate the interconnectedness of all living things and to recognise our role as stewards of this delicate balance.

Companion Planting for Pest Control

Companion planting is a time-honoured technique that harnesses the natural relationships between plants to create a healthier and more balanced garden. By strategically interplanting different species, we can deter pests, attract beneficial insects, and improve the overall health and productivity of our plants. It's a subtle art, a dance of aromas and root exudates, where we act as choreographers, guiding the interactions between plants to create a harmonious and resilient ecosystem.

Companion planting works on several principles. Some plants release volatile compounds that repel pests, confusing them or masking the scent of their preferred host plants. Others attract beneficial insects that prey on pests or parasitise them, acting as natural bodyguards for our crops. Some plants improve the growth or flavour of their neighbours, perhaps by enhancing nutrient uptake or providing shade from the harsh sun. Still others provide physical support or act as living trellises for climbing companions. By understanding these principles, we can create plant partnerships that benefit both species and contribute to a more resilient garden ecosystem.

There are countless examples of beneficial plant combinations, each with its own unique story to tell. Planting marigolds alongside tomatoes can deter whiteflies and nematodes, their pungent aroma masking the scent of the tomato plants. Growing basil near peppers can improve their flavour and growth, while also repelling aphids and spider mites. Interplanting onions and carrots can confuse carrot root flies, making it harder for them to locate their preferred host. Planting nasturtiums near beans can attract aphids away from the bean plants, acting as a sacrificial crop to protect the more valuable beans. Experimenting with different combinations in your own garden can reveal surprising and beneficial relationships, adding another layer of fascination to the gardening experience.

Companion planting is just one tool in the arsenal of creating a pest-resistant garden. Healthy soil, teeming with beneficial microbes and organic matter, provides the foundation for strong and resilient plants. Diverse plantings, with a variety of species and growth habits, create a more complex ecosystem that is less susceptible to pest outbreaks. Providing habitats for beneficial insects, such as ladybugs, lacewings, and hoverflies, ensures that natural predators are on hand to keep pest populations in check. By focusing on preventative measures and natural pest control methods, we can minimise the need for harmful pesticides and create a garden that is both productive and ecologically sound.

Beyond Pest Control: The Magic of Plant Partnerships

Companion planting extends far beyond simply deterring pests. It delves into the fascinating world of plant interactions, where subtle chemical signals and root exudates create a complex web of relationships. Some plants, like chamomile, are said to improve the flavour of their neighbours, such as cucumbers and melons, when planted nearby. Others, like yarrow, can enhance the essential oil content of herbs like lavender and rosemary. Exploring these subtle relationships can add a new dimension to your gardening experience and lead to surprising discoveries.

The Science of Companion Planting

The effectiveness of companion planting has been debated for centuries, but recent research has shed light on the scientific basis for many of these traditional practices. Allelopathy, the chemical inhibition of one plant by another, plays a role in some companion planting combinations. For example, the roots of black walnut trees release juglone, a substance that inhibits the growth of many other plants. Plants also release volatile organic compounds (VOCs) that can affect their neighbours. These VOCs can act as attractants for beneficial insects or repellents for pests. Understanding these underlying mechanisms can help us make more informed choices about plant combinations in our gardens.

Specific Examples of Companion Planting

Here are some more specific examples of beneficial plant combinations, categorised by plant families or garden areas:

Brassicas: Interplanting brassicas like cabbage and broccoli with aromatic herbs like rosemary and thyme can help deter cabbage white butterflies. The strong scent of the herbs masks the scent of the brassicas, making it harder for the butterflies to locate them.

Legumes: Legumes like peas and beans fix nitrogen in the soil, benefiting neighbouring plants. Planting them near nitrogen-loving crops like corn or squash can improve their growth. This is a classic example of a mutually beneficial relationship, known as the "Three Sisters" planting method.

Alliums: Alliums like onions and garlic have strong scents that can deter many pests. Planting them near carrots can help deter carrot root flies, while planting them near roses can help prevent black spot.

Nightshades: Planting basil near tomatoes and peppers can improve their flavour and growth, while also repelling aphids and spider mites.

Common Companion Planting Mistakes
While companion planting can be a valuable tool, it's important to avoid some common mistakes:

Planting Incompatible Species: Not all plants get along. Some plants release substances that inhibit the growth of others. For example, planting potatoes near tomatoes can increase the risk of blight, as both are susceptible to the same disease.

Overcrowding Plants: Even beneficial plant combinations can suffer if they are overcrowded. Ensure that each plant has adequate space to grow and access sunlight and nutrients.

Ignoring Other Factors: Companion planting is just one aspect of creating a healthy garden. Don't neglect other important factors, such as soil health, watering, and providing habitats for beneficial insects.

April Gardening Tasks
April is a month of rapid growth and development in the garden. We must be attentive to the needs of our plants, providing them with the support and care they need to thrive.

Planting Summer-Flowering Bulbs: April is the ideal time to plant summer-flowering bulbs, such as lilies, dahlias, and gladioli. Choose a sunny location with well-drained soil. Plant the bulbs at the correct depth, ensuring that the tips are just below the soil surface. Water well and mulch to retain moisture.

Lilies: There are many different types of lilies, each with its own unique beauty and planting requirements. Asiatic lilies are among the easiest to grow, while Oriental lilies are known for their fragrance. Trumpet lilies have large, trumpet-shaped flowers, while Turk's cap lilies have reflexed petals and intricate patterns. Choose lilies that are suited to your climate and soil conditions.

Dahlias: Dahlias are a favourite for their stunning variety of colours and forms. Choose healthy tubers with visible eyes or sprouts. Prepare the soil by adding compost or well-rotted manure. Plant the tubers horizontally, about 4-6 inches deep, with the eyes facing upwards. Provide support for their tall stems with stakes or cages.

Gladioli: Gladioli produce tall spikes of colourful blooms that add vertical interest to the garden. Plant the corms about 4-6 inches deep and 6-8 inches apart. To ensure a continuous display of blooms throughout the summer, stagger your plantings, planting a few corms every couple of weeks.

Thinning Seedlings: If you've sown seeds directly into the ground or started them indoors, it's important to thin the seedlings to give them adequate space to grow. Thinning prevents overcrowding and competition for resources, resulting in stronger and healthier plants. Follow the spacing recommendations on the seed packet. You can transplant thinned seedlings to other areas of the garden or pot them up to give away or grow elsewhere.

Root crops: Thinning root crops like carrots and beets is particularly important to ensure proper root development. Overcrowding can lead to stunted growth and deformed roots. Thin the seedlings to the recommended spacing, leaving the strongest and healthiest plants in place.

Lettuce: Lettuce can be thinned in stages to create a continuous supply of fresh leaves. Start by thinning the seedlings to about an inch apart. As they grow, thin them again to their final spacing, using the thinnings for salads.

Providing Support for Climbing Plants: Climbing plants, such as peas, beans, and cucumbers, need support to grow vertically. Install trellises, netting, or other support structures before the plants start to climb. This will prevent them from sprawling on the ground and becoming tangled, which can lead to disease and reduced yields.

Trellises: Trellises come in a variety of styles, from simple A-frames to elaborate obelisks. Choose a trellis that is appropriate for the size and vigour of the plant you are growing. For example, a sturdy trellis is needed for heavy vining crops like cucumbers and melons, while a lighter trellis is sufficient for peas and beans.

Netting: Netting can be used to support vining crops like cucumbers and melons. Attach the netting to sturdy posts or a fence. As the plants grow, guide their tendrils through the netting to help them climb.

Natural Supports: You can also use other plants as natural supports for climbing plants. For example, corn stalks can be used to support.

May

Sun	Mon	Tue	Wed	Thu	Fri	Sat
				1	2	3
4	5	6	7	8	9	10
11	12	13	14	15	15	17
18	19	20	21	22	25	22
28	26	27	28	30		

38

Chapter 5: Abundant Blooms (May)

May arrives, a crescendo of vibrant life and intoxicating scents. The garden is a symphony of buzzing bees, fluttering butterflies, and the melodies of birdsong. Abundant blooms adorn every corner, a testament to the flourishing ecosystem we've nurtured. This is a time to revel in the beauty we've created, to observe the intricate web of life unfolding before our eyes, and to continue our journey towards a truly biodiverse sanctuary.

Supporting Wildlife

Creating a wildlife-friendly garden is about more than just providing food and shelter. It's about creating a haven where creatures can thrive, where they can raise their young, and where they can contribute to the delicate balance of the ecosystem. It's about fostering a sense of wonder and connection with the natural world, reminding ourselves that we are part of something larger than ourselves.

A truly wildlife-friendly garden caters to the needs of a diverse range of creatures. It provides a variety of food sources, from nectar-rich flowers for pollinators to berry-laden shrubs for birds. It offers shelter in the form of dense hedges, log piles, and nesting boxes. It provides access to water, whether it's a simple birdbath or a more elaborate pond. And it avoids the use of harmful pesticides and chemicals that can disrupt the delicate balance of the ecosystem.

Think about the different layers within your garden and how each can support various forms of life. Tall trees provide nesting sites for birds, squirrels, and even bats. The understory, with its shrubs and smaller trees, offers shelter and nesting sites for a wider range of birds, butterflies, and small mammals.

The herbaceous layer, with its flowering plants, grasses, and groundcovers, provides nectar and pollen for pollinators, while also offering shelter for insects and small mammals. Even the ground layer, with its leaf litter, logs, and stones, provides a vital habitat for insects, amphibians, and reptiles.

Incorporate features that specifically cater to wildlife. Log piles provide refuge for hedgehogs, insects, and amphibians. Rock piles offer basking spots for reptiles and shelter for insects. Compost heaps provide a warm and moist environment for insects and other decomposers, contributing to the recycling of nutrients within the garden. Water features, from simple birdbaths to more elaborate ponds, attract a wide range of wildlife for drinking and bathing.

Remember the crucial role of native plants in supporting local wildlife. Native plants have co-evolved with local insects, birds, and other animals, providing them with the ideal food and habitat. They are perfectly adapted to the local climate and soil conditions, requiring less maintenance and fewer inputs. Incorporate native plants into your garden to create a truly authentic and sustainable ecosystem.

While we strive to create a welcoming environment for wildlife, we may encounter creatures that are considered pests, such as deer, rabbits, or squirrels. Instead of resorting to harmful chemicals or traps, consider humane and environmentally friendly solutions. Fencing can protect vulnerable plants, while repellents can deter unwanted visitors. Providing alternative food sources, such as planting a sacrificial crop of clover or sunflowers to attract deer away from your prized roses, can also be effective.

Attracting Birds, Butterflies, and Other Beneficial Creatures

Each creature has its own unique needs and preferences. Birds are attracted to gardens that offer a variety of food sources, such as seeds, berries, and insects. They also need safe places to nest and raise their young, such as dense shrubs, trees, or nesting boxes.

Butterflies are drawn to nectar-rich flowers in sunny locations. They also need host plants for their caterpillars, such as nettles for the peacock butterfly or milkweed for the monarch butterfly.

Other beneficial creatures, such as hedgehogs, frogs, and toads, play a vital role in controlling pests and maintaining a healthy ecosystem. Providing them with shelter in the form of log piles, compost heaps, or purpose-built shelters can encourage them to make your garden their home.

Building Birdhouses and Nesting Boxes

Providing nesting sites for birds can significantly increase their presence in your garden and contribute to their conservation. Choose birdhouses or nesting boxes that are appropriate for the species you want to attract. Consider the size of the entrance hole, the dimensions of the box, and the preferred nesting materials.

Place them in sheltered locations, away from predators and harsh weather conditions. Face them away from prevailing winds and direct sunlight. Clean them out regularly at the end of the nesting season to prevent the buildup of parasites and diseases.

May Gardening Tasks

May is a busy month in the garden, a time to plant, nurture, and protect the burgeoning life that surrounds us.

- **Planting out tender seedlings:** As the danger of frost passes, it's time to plant out tender seedlings, such as tomatoes, peppers, and cucumbers. Harden them off gradually before planting them in their final positions. Choose a sunny location with fertile, well-drained soil. Water regularly and provide support for vining plants.

  - **Tomatoes:** There are countless tomato varieties to choose from, each with its own unique flavour, size, and growth habit. Determinate tomatoes are bush-type plants that produce a single crop, while indeterminate tomatoes are vining plants that produce fruit throughout the season. Cherry tomatoes are small and sweet, while beefsteak tomatoes are large and meaty. Choose varieties that are suited to your climate and taste preferences.

  - **Peppers:** Peppers come in a wide range of flavours, from sweet bell peppers to fiery chili peppers. Plant them in a sunny location with well-drained soil. Provide support for their stems with stakes or cages, especially for taller varieties.

  - **Cucumbers:** Cucumbers are vigorous climbers that need plenty of space to grow. Train them to climb a trellis or fence to save space and improve air circulation. Water regularly and mulch to retain moisture. To prevent powdery mildew, avoid overhead watering and provide good air circulation.

- **Mulching to conserve moisture and suppress weeds:** Mulching is an essential gardening practice that helps to conserve moisture, suppress weeds, and improve soil health. Apply a layer of organic mulch, such as compost, bark chips, or straw, around your plants. This will help to keep the soil cool and moist, reducing the need for watering. It will also prevent weed seeds from germinating and competing with your plants for resources.

    - **Wood chips:** Wood chips are a long-lasting mulch that is effective at suppressing weeds. They are ideal for use around trees and shrubs.

    - **Straw:** Straw is a good choice for vegetable gardens, as it helps to keep the soil cool and moist. It decomposes quickly, adding organic matter to the soil.

    - **Compost:** Compost is an excellent mulch that adds nutrients to the soil and improves its structure. It is ideal for use around all types of plants.

- **Monitoring for pests and diseases:** Regular monitoring for pests and diseases is crucial to prevent outbreaks and protect your plants. Inspect your plants regularly for signs of damage or unusual growth. Identify any pests or diseases early and take appropriate action. Encourage natural predators, such as ladybugs and lacewings, to help control pest populations. Use organic pest control methods whenever possible to avoid harming beneficial insects and disrupting the delicate balance of the ecosystem.

- **Aphids:** Aphids are small, sap-sucking insects that can weaken plants and transmit diseases. Encourage natural predators like ladybugs and lacewings to control aphid populations. You can also use organic control methods like insecticidal soap or neem oil.
- **Slugs and snails:** Slugs and snails can cause significant damage to plants, especially young seedlings. Prevent slug and snail damage by using barriers, such as copper tape or diatomaceous earth. You can also trap them with beer traps or attract natural predators like hedgehogs and birds.
- **Powdery mildew:** Powdery mildew is a fungal disease that appears as a white powdery coating on leaves. Prevent powdery mildew by providing good air circulation and avoiding overhead watering. You can also use organic fungicides like milk or baking soda solutions.

Featured Plant: Lavender (Lavandula spp.)
Lavender is a beloved herb, cherished for its fragrant flowers, culinary uses, and therapeutic properties. It's also a valuable addition to any biodiversity garden, attracting a wide range of pollinators, including bees, butterflies, and hoverflies.

Lavender thrives in sunny locations with well-drained soil. It's drought-tolerant and relatively low-maintenance, making it an ideal choice for busy gardeners. The flowers can be harvested and dried for use in sachets, potpourri, or culinary creations. Lavender is also known for its calming and relaxing properties, making it a popular ingredient in aromatherapy products.

Recipe: Lavender Lemonade

This refreshing lemonade is infused with the delicate floral aroma of lavender.

Ingredients:
- 1 cup sugar
- 1 cup water
- 1 cup fresh lavender flowers
- 1 cup lemon juice
- 7 cups cold water

Instructions:
1. Combine the sugar and 1 cup of water in a saucepan. Bring to a boil, stirring until the sugar dissolves.
2. Add the lavender flowers to the sugar syrup and remove from heat. Let steep for 30 minutes.
3. Strain the lavender syrup into a pitcher.
4. Add the lemon juice and 7 cups of cold water to the pitcher.
5. Stir well and serve over ice.

Chapter 6: Summer Harvest (June)

June arrives, a month of long sunny days and the promise of abundant harvests. The garden is a riot of colour and fragrance, a testament to the resilience and diversity we've fostered. It's a time to celebrate the fruits of our labour, to savour the flavours of sun-ripened produce, and to continue our vigilance in maintaining a balanced and thriving ecosystem. As the garden reaches its peak, we must be mindful of the challenges that lie ahead, particularly the ever-present threat of pests seeking to share in the abundance we've cultivated.

Organic Pest Control: A Holistic Approach

Even in the most biodiverse and well-managed gardens, pests can occasionally appear, threatening to disrupt the harmony we've carefully cultivated. But fear not, for nature provides a wealth of solutions to keep these unwelcome visitors in check without resorting to harmful chemicals that can harm beneficial insects, pollute the environment, and compromise the health of our soil. Organic pest control is not just about eliminating pests; it's about understanding the complex web of life in our gardens and working with nature to maintain a healthy balance.

The first step in organic pest control is to identify the culprits. Familiarise yourself with the common pests in your region and learn to recognise their telltale signs. Aphids, with their tiny pear-shaped bodies and insatiable appetite for plant sap, can cause distorted growth and weaken plants. Slugs and snails leave a trail of slime and chewed leaves in their wake, particularly favouring tender young seedlings.

Cabbage white butterflies lay their eggs on brassicas, and their voracious caterpillars can decimate entire crops. Spider mites, tiny arachnids that are barely visible to the naked eye, can cause stippling and yellowing of leaves. By recognising these pests and understanding their life cycles, we can take proactive steps to prevent infestations and minimize their impact.

Knowing the life cycle of a pest is crucial for effective control. For example, understanding that aphids reproduce rapidly in warm weather can help us anticipate infestations and take preventative measures, such as introducing natural predators or using deterrent sprays. Knowing that cabbage white butterflies lay their eggs on the underside of leaves can help us target our control efforts, such as handpicking the eggs or using netting to prevent the butterflies from accessing the plants.

Nature offers a wealth of tools for controlling pests without resorting to harmful chemicals. Handpicking is a simple yet effective method for removing larger pests like caterpillars and slugs. It's a mindful practice that allows us to connect with our plants and observe the subtle signs of pest activity. Encourage natural predators, such as ladybugs, lacewings, and birds, by providing them with suitable habitats and avoiding the use of pesticides.

Plant a diversity of flowering plants to attract beneficial insects and provide nesting sites for birds. Introduce biological controls, such as nematodes or parasitic wasps, to target specific pests. These natural enemies can help to keep pest populations in check without harming other organisms. Create natural sprays using ingredients like garlic, chili peppers, or neem oil to deter pests and protect your plants. These sprays can be effective against a wide range of pests, and they are safe for humans, pets, and the environment.

Harmful pesticides not only kill pests but also harm beneficial insects, pollinators, and soil organisms. They can contaminate water sources and pose risks to human and animal health. By avoiding these chemicals and embracing organic pest control methods, we can create a healthier and more sustainable garden ecosystem. Remember that a healthy garden is a balanced ecosystem, and a few pests are a natural part of that balance. Our goal is not to eliminate all pests but to manage their populations and prevent them from causing significant damage.

Building a Healthy Soil Ecosystem

Healthy soil is the foundation of a thriving garden and a key component of organic pest control. A healthy soil ecosystem is teeming with beneficial microbes, fungi, and other organisms that help to suppress pests and diseases. These organisms compete with pests for resources, produce antibiotics that kill harmful microbes, and help to break down organic matter, releasing nutrients that strengthen plants.

To build healthy soil, incorporate plenty of organic matter, such as compost, leaf mold, or well-rotted manure. Avoid tilling the soil excessively, as this can disrupt the soil structure and harm beneficial organisms. Use cover crops to protect the soil and add nutrients. And avoid the use of synthetic fertilizers and pesticides, which can harm soil organisms and disrupt the delicate balance of the soil ecosystem.

Encouraging Biodiversity

A diverse garden is a more resilient garden. Planting a variety of plants, including flowers, herbs, and vegetables, creates a more complex ecosystem that is less susceptible to pest outbreaks. Different plants attract different beneficial insects, creating a natural army of pest control agents. A diverse garden also provides a wider range of food sources and habitats for wildlife, contributing to the overall health and biodiversity of your garden.

June Gardening Tasks

June is a month of abundance, a time to reap the rewards of our spring labours and enjoy the fruits (and vegetables!) of our efforts.

- **Harvesting early summer crops:** Early summer crops, such as lettuce, spinach, radishes, and peas, are ready for harvest. Harvest regularly to encourage continued production and prevent plants from bolting or going to seed. Enjoy the fresh flavours of your homegrown produce and consider preserving any surplus for later use. You can freeze, can, or dry your produce to enjoy it throughout the year.

- **Watering regularly during dry periods:** As temperatures rise and rainfall becomes less frequent, it's crucial to water your plants regularly, especially those that are newly planted or growing in containers. Water deeply and less frequently to encourage deep root growth. Water early in the morning or late in the evening to minimise evaporation. Use a watering can or a soaker hose to deliver water directly to the roots of your plants, avoiding wetting the leaves, which can encourage fungal diseases.

- **Deadheading flowers to encourage more blooms:** Deadheading, or removing spent flowers, encourages plants to produce more blooms and extends their flowering season. It also prevents plants from putting energy into seed production, which can reduce their overall vigour. Deadheading can be done by simply pinching off the faded flowers or using pruning shears to remove the entire flower stalk.

Featured Plant: Nasturtium (Tropaeolum majus)
Nasturtiums are cheerful and versatile annuals that are not only a feast for the eyes but also valuable companions in the garden. Their vibrant flowers attract pollinators, while their peppery leaves and flowers add a zesty touch to salads and other culinary creations.

Nasturtiums are also known for their pest-repellent properties, deterring aphids, whiteflies, and other unwanted visitors. They are easy to grow, thriving in full sun and well-drained soil. Plant them among your vegetables to add colour, attract beneficial insects, and deter pests. Nasturtiums are also edible, and their leaves and flowers can be used to add a peppery bite to salads, sandwiches, and other dishes.

Recipe: Nasturtium Pesto
This vibrant pesto is a delicious way to use nasturtium leaves and flowers.
Ingredients:
- 1 cup packed nasturtium leaves
- 1/2 cup grated Parmesan cheese
- 1/4 cup pine nuts
- 2 cloves garlic
- 1/2 cup olive oil
- Salt and pepper to taste

Instructions:
1. Combine the nasturtium leaves, Parmesan cheese, pine nuts, and garlic in a food processor.
2. Pulse until finely chopped.
3. With the food processor running, slowly drizzle in the olive oil until a smooth paste forms.
4. Season with salt and pepper to taste.
5. Serve with pasta, bread, or vegetables.

Garden Journal Prompt:
Reflect on the challenges and successes you've experienced in your garden this year. What lessons have you learned about organic pest control and maintaining a balanced ecosystem? How can you apply these lessons to future gardening endeavours? Record your thoughts and observations in your journal.

June is a month of abundance and fulfilment, a time to savour the fruits of our labour and appreciate the intricate web of life that thrives in our gardens. By embracing organic pest control methods and continuing to nurture our garden ecosystems, we can create a haven for both plants and wildlife, a sanctuary where we can connect with the natural world and find solace in its rhythms.

Chapter 7: Peak Season (July)

July arrives, a month of long, sun-drenched days and the culmination of our gardening efforts. The garden is a vibrant tapestry of textures and colours, a testament to the biodiversity we've nurtured. It's a time to revel in the abundance of the season, to savour the fruits of our labour, and to appreciate the intricate web of life that thrives under our care. But as the sun beats down and temperatures soar, we must also be mindful of the challenges that July brings, particularly the need to conserve water and protect our plants from heat stress.

This month requires a shift in our gardening approach, a move towards strategies that prioritise resilience and sustainability in the face of summer's intensity.

Water Conservation in the Garden: A Precious Resource
Water is a precious resource, and as responsible gardeners, we must use it wisely, especially during the hot summer months. By implementing water-wise gardening practices, we can reduce our reliance on mains water, conserve this vital resource, and create a more sustainable garden ecosystem.

It's a matter of respecting the natural cycles of water, understanding how it moves through the landscape, and working with nature to ensure its availability for all living things.

- **Implementing water-wise gardening practices:** There are many ways to conserve water in the garden, each contributing to a more sustainable and resilient ecosystem. Start by choosing plants that are well-suited to your climate and soil conditions.

- Drought-tolerant plants, such as lavender, rosemary, and sedums, require less water than thirsty plants like hydrangeas and hostas. These plants have evolved strategies to cope with dry conditions, such as smaller leaves, waxy coatings, or deep root systems that help them access moisture deeper in the soil. Group plants with similar water needs together to avoid overwatering some while underwatering others. This creates microclimates within the garden, where plants can thrive in conditions that suit their individual needs.

- **Watering techniques:** Water deeply and less frequently to encourage deep root growth, which helps plants access moisture deeper in the soil. Shallow watering encourages shallow root growth, making plants more susceptible to drought stress. Water early in the morning or late in the evening to minimise evaporation. The cooler temperatures and reduced wind at these times allow the water to penetrate the soil more effectively. Use a watering can with a fine rose or a soaker hose to deliver water directly to the roots of your plants, avoiding wetting the leaves, which can encourage fungal diseases.

- **Mulching and soil improvement:** Mulch acts as a protective blanket over the soil, reducing evaporation and keeping the soil cool and moist. Organic mulches, such as compost, bark chips, or straw, also improve soil health as they decompose, adding organic matter and nutrients to the soil. Improving soil health is crucial for water conservation. Healthy soil, with its good structure and abundance of organic matter, acts like a sponge, absorbing and retaining water more effectively. This reduces runoff and ensures that water is available to plants when they need it.

- **Collecting rainwater:** Rainwater is a valuable resource that is often wasted. By installing a rain barrel or other rainwater harvesting system, we can collect and store rainwater for use in the garden. Rainwater is naturally soft and free of chlorine and other chemicals found in tap water, making it ideal for plants. It can be used to water plants, fill ponds, or even wash garden tools. Rainwater harvesting not only conserves water but also reduces our reliance on mains water, which is often treated with chemicals and requires energy to pump and distribute.

Choosing the Right Plants for a Water-Wise Garden
Selecting plants that are well-suited to your climate and soil conditions is crucial for creating a water-wise garden. Consider the following factors when choosing plants:

- **Drought tolerance:** Choose plants that are known for their drought tolerance, such as lavender, rosemary, sedums, and ornamental grasses. These plants can thrive with minimal watering, especially once established.

- **Native plants:** Native plants are naturally adapted to the local climate and soil conditions, making them ideal for water-wise gardens. They require less water and are more resistant to pests and diseases.

- **Leaf size and shape:** Plants with smaller leaves or waxy coatings tend to lose less water through transpiration. Succulents, with their thick, fleshy leaves, are particularly adept at storing water.

- **Root systems:** Plants with deep root systems can access water deeper in the soil, making them more drought tolerant.

Creating Microclimates in the Garden
By strategically placing plants and other garden features, we can create microclimates that help to conserve water and protect plants from heat stress. For example, planting tall trees or shrubs on the south or west side of the garden can provide shade for more delicate plants.

Creating a windbreak with hedges or fences can reduce water loss through transpiration. And grouping plants with similar water needs together can help to ensure that each plant receives the appropriate amount of water.

July Gardening Tasks
July is a month of abundance, a time to harvest the fruits of our labour and enjoy the bounty of the garden. But it's also a time to be vigilant, protecting our plants from the stresses of summer heat and ensuring a continuous supply of fresh produce.

- **Harvesting summer fruits and vegetables:** Summer fruits and vegetables, such as tomatoes, peppers, cucumbers, beans, and berries, are at their peak in July. Harvest regularly to encourage continued production and prevent fruits and vegetables from becoming overripe. Enjoy the fresh flavours of your homegrown produce and consider preserving any surplus for later use. You can freeze, can, or dry your produce to enjoy it throughout the year.

- **Succession planting for continuous harvests:** To ensure a continuous supply of fresh produce throughout the summer, consider succession planting. This involves sowing small batches of seeds or planting seedlings every few weeks. This way, you'll have a continuous harvest of your favourite crops, such as lettuce, radishes, and carrots. Succession planting not only provides a continuous supply of fresh produce but also helps to prevent gluts, where you have too much of one crop at a time.

- **Protecting plants from heat stress:** High temperatures and intense sunlight can stress plants, leading to wilting, sunscald, and reduced yields. Provide shade for vulnerable plants during the hottest part of the day. Water regularly, especially during dry periods. Mulch to keep the soil cool and moist. And consider using shade cloth or row covers to protect plants from intense sunlight. You can also mist plants with water to cool them down during hot weather.

Featured Plant: Sunflower (Helianthus annuus)
Sunflowers are iconic symbols of summer, their cheerful faces following the sun across the sky. These towering plants are not only a delight to behold but also valuable contributors to the biodiversity of the garden. Their nectar-rich flowers attract a wide range of pollinators, including bees, butterflies, and hoverflies. Their seeds provide food for birds and other wildlife. And their tall stems offer support for climbing plants.

Sunflowers are easy to grow, thriving in full sun and well-drained soil. They come in a variety of sizes and colours, from dwarf varieties that reach just a few feet tall to giant varieties that can tower over ten feet. Sunflowers are also a valuable source of food for humans, and their seeds can be roasted and eaten as a snack or used to make sunflower oil.

DIY Project: Building a Rain Barrel
Creating a rain barrel is a simple and rewarding way to conserve water, reduce your reliance on municipal supplies, and provide your garden with a natural source of irrigation. It's a practical step towards sustainability, allowing you to harness the power of rainfall and contribute to a healthier environment.

Materials:
- **Recycled plastic drum or food-grade barrel:** Choose a container with a capacity of at least 50 gallons. Make sure it's food-grade to avoid any potential contamination of the water.
- **Lid:** A tight-fitting lid will prevent debris and mosquitoes from entering the barrel.
- **Downspout diverter:** This device directs water from your downspout into the rain barrel.
- **Spigot or hose bib:** For easy access to the collected water.
- **Overflow hose:** To direct excess water away from your foundation.
- **Mesh screen or window screening:** To prevent debris and mosquitoes from entering the barrel.
- **Silicone sealant or caulk:** To seal any openings and prevent leaks.
- **Drill with hole saw attachments:** For creating holes for the spigot and overflow hose.
- **Screws or bolts:** For attaching the spigot and overflow hose.
- **Teflon tape:** To ensure a watertight seal around the spigot and overflow hose.
- **Optional:** Bricks or cinder blocks to elevate the barrel and improve water pressure.

Instructions:
1. **Prepare the barrel:** Thoroughly clean the barrel with soap and water to remove any residue. Rinse well and let it dry completely.
2. **Install the spigot:**
    - Choose a location for the spigot near the bottom of the barrel.
    - Use a hole saw attachment to drill a hole the size of the spigot.
    - Apply silicone sealant or caulk around the hole.
    - Insert the spigot into the hole and secure it with screws or bolts.
    - Wrap Teflon tape around the threads of the spigot to ensure a watertight seal.

- **Install the overflow hose:**
    - Choose a location for the overflow hose near the top of the barrel.
    - Use a hole saw attachment to drill a hole the size of the overflow hose.
    - Apply silicone sealant or caulk around the hole.
    - Insert the overflow hose into the hole and secure it with screws or bolts.
    - Wrap Teflon tape around the threads of the overflow hose to ensure a watertight seal.
- **Prepare the lid:**
    - Cut a hole in the lid for the downspout diverter.
    - Attach the mesh screen or window screening to the underside of the lid to prevent debris and mosquitoes from entering the barrel.
- **Connect the downspout diverter:**
    - Install the downspout diverter on your downspout, directing water into the rain barrel.
    - Ensure that the diverter is positioned to allow excess water to flow out of the downspout and away from your foundation.
3. **Elevate the barrel (optional):** Place the rain barrel on bricks or cinder blocks to elevate it and improve water pressure. This will make it easier to use a watering can or hose to access the water.
4. **Test the system:** Wait for a rainfall and check that the rain barrel is collecting water properly. Ensure that the spigot and overflow hose are working correctly and that there are no leaks.

Tips for Rain Barrel Success:
- **Choose a location:** Place the rain barrel near a downspout that receives adequate rainfall.
- **Maintain the barrel:** Clean the rain barrel periodically to prevent the buildup of debris and algae.

- **Winterise the barrel:** In colder climates, disconnect the downspout diverter and empty the rain barrel before winter to prevent freezing and damage.
- **Use the water wisely:** Use the collected rainwater to water your garden, wash your car, or for other non-potable uses.

Additional Ideas:
- **Connect multiple rain barrels:** Increase your water storage capacity by connecting multiple rain barrels together.
- **Install a filter:** Install a filter to remove debris and improve water quality.
- **Paint the barrel:** Paint the barrel to match your house or garden décor.
- **Add a planter on top:** Create a beautiful and functional feature by adding a planter on top of the rain barrel.

By building a rain barrel, you not only contribute to a more sustainable environment but also gain a valuable resource for your garden. Enjoy the satisfaction of harvesting nature's bounty and using it to nurture the life in your garden.

Garden Journal Prompt:
Reflect on your water usage in the garden. How can you further reduce your reliance on mains water? What water-wise gardening practices can you implement? Record your thoughts and observations in your journal.

July is a month of abundance and vibrancy, a time to celebrate the peak of the gardening season and appreciate the interconnectedness of life in our gardens. By embracing water conservation methods and protecting our plants from the stresses of summer, we can ensure a healthy and productive garden that continues to thrive throughout the season.

Chapter 8: Late Summer Bounty (August)

August arrives, a month of ripening fruits, swelling vegetables, and the sweet aroma of summer's bounty. The garden is a vibrant tapestry of life, a testament to the careful nurturing and the harmonious balance we've fostered. It's a time to celebrate the abundance of the season, to savour the flavours of sun-ripened tomatoes and juicy berries, and to gather the seeds that will carry our gardening legacy into the future.

However, even as we revel in the present abundance, we must also look ahead, preparing for the transition to autumn and ensuring the continued health and vitality of our garden ecosystem. This is a time to reflect on the journey we've taken, to appreciate the lessons we've learned, and to embrace the cyclical nature of the gardening year.

Seed Saving: Preserving Our Garden Heritage
Seed saving is an ancient practice, a way of connecting with the past and ensuring the future of our gardens. It's a way of preserving the unique characteristics of our favourite plants, adapting them to our specific growing conditions, and sharing our passion for gardening with future generations.

It's a simple yet profound act that empowers us to become active participants in the cycle of life, a way of honouring the legacy of those who came before us and contributing to the well-being of those who will follow.

Not all plants are created equal when it comes to seed saving. Choose open-pollinated varieties, also known as heirloom varieties, which will produce offspring that are true to the parent plant. These varieties have been passed down through generations, carrying with them a rich history and a unique genetic heritage.

Hybrid varieties, on the other hand, are often sterile or produce offspring with unpredictable traits. Select the healthiest and most vigorous plants for seed saving, ensuring that they exhibit the desired characteristics, such as flavour, size, or disease resistance. Allow the fruits or seed pods to fully mature on the plant before harvesting. This ensures that the seeds are fully developed and have the best chance of germinating. Extract the seeds carefully, removing any pulp or debris. And be sure to label the seeds clearly with the plant name, variety, and date of harvest. This information will be invaluable when you sow the seeds in future seasons.

Seed saving is not just about collecting seeds; it's about selecting the best seeds to ensure the continued health and vigour of your plants. Look for plants that are disease-free, productive, and exhibit the desired characteristics. For example, if you're saving tomato seeds, choose fruits from plants that have produced abundant, flavourful tomatoes and have shown resistance to diseases. This careful selection process helps to improve the quality of your seeds and ensures that your plants continue to thrive.

Proper storage is crucial for maintaining seed viability. Dry the seeds thoroughly before storing them to prevent mold and decay. Spread them out on a clean, dry surface in a well-ventilated area. Avoid exposing them to direct sunlight. Store them in a cool, dark, and dry place, such as a refrigerator or a dedicated seed storage box. Use airtight containers to prevent moisture and pests from damaging the seeds. Glass jars or plastic containers with tight-fitting lids are ideal. And consider storing seeds in multiple locations to safeguard against loss or damage. This ensures that you have a backup supply in case of unforeseen circumstances.

Assemble a basic toolkit for seed saving. This might include small scissors or tweezers for carefully removing seeds from pods or fruits, a fine mesh sieve for rinsing seeds and removing debris, paper envelopes or bags for storing dried seeds, labels and a pen for labelling seeds with the plant name, variety, and date of harvest, and airtight containers for long-term storage of seeds.

Seed banks and exchanges play a vital role in preserving plant diversity and ensuring the availability of seeds for future generations. Consider donating some of your saved seeds to a local seed bank or participating in a seed exchange. This is a wonderful way to share your passion for gardening, connect with other gardeners, and contribute to the preservation of our garden heritage. Seed banks act as repositories for seeds, safeguarding them against loss and ensuring their availability for future generations. Seed exchanges provide a platform for gardeners to share and trade seeds, promoting diversity and fostering a sense of community.

August Gardening Tasks
August is a month of transition, a time to harvest the abundance of summer while preparing for the cooler days of autumn. Harvesting and preserving the abundance of summer produce is a key task in August, which is the peak of the harvest season for many fruits and vegetables, including tomatoes, peppers, cucumbers, beans, squash, and berries.

Harvest regularly to encourage continued production and prevent produce from becoming overripe. Enjoy the fresh flavours of your homegrown produce and consider preserving any surplus for later use. You can freeze, can, or dry your produce to enjoy it throughout the year. Experiment with different preservation methods, such as making jams, jellies, pickles, or sauces. This is a wonderful way to capture the flavours of summer and enjoy them throughout the year.

Start preparing your garden beds for fall planting. Remove spent crops and weeds. Amend the soil with compost or other organic matter to replenish nutrients and improve soil health. Consider planting cover crops, such as clover or rye, to protect the soil and add nutrients over the winter. Cover crops help to prevent soil erosion, suppress weeds, and improve soil fertility. They also provide habitat for beneficial insects and other wildlife.

Remove spent crops to prevent the spread of pests and diseases. Compost healthy plant debris to recycle nutrients and reduce waste. If you suspect any diseased plants, dispose of them carefully to avoid contaminating other areas of the garden. You can also chop and drop spent crops, leaving them on the soil surface to decompose and add organic matter.

Featured Plant: Tomato (Solanum Lycopersicum)
Tomatoes are a staple of the summer garden, their juicy fruits bursting with flavour and versatility. They come in a bewildering array of shapes, sizes, and colours, from tiny cherry tomatoes to hefty beefsteak tomatoes, from vibrant red to sunny yellow and deep purple.

Tomatoes are relatively easy to grow, thriving in full sun and fertile, well-drained soil. They require regular watering, especially during dry periods, and benefit from support to keep their fruits off the ground. Tomatoes are also excellent candidates for seed saving, allowing you to preserve your favourite varieties and adapt them to your specific growing conditions.

Seed Saving Tips for Tomatoes:
- Choose open-pollinated varieties for seed saving.
- Select healthy, ripe fruits from vigorous plants.
- Scoop out the seeds and pulp and place them in a jar.
- Add a small amount of water and let the mixture ferment for a few days.

- This process helps to remove the gel coating around the seeds and prevent the spread of diseases.
- Rinse the seeds thoroughly and spread them out to dry on a paper towel.
- Store the dried seeds in a cool, dark, and dry place.

Recipe: Tomato Sauce

This simple tomato sauce captures the essence of summer's bounty.

Ingredients:
- 4 pounds ripe tomatoes, chopped
- 1 onion, chopped
- 2 cloves garlic, minced
- 1/4 cup olive oil
- 1 teaspoon dried oregano
- Salt and pepper to taste

Instructions:
1. Heat the olive oil in a large saucepan over medium heat.
2. Add the onion and garlic and cook until softened, about 5 minutes.
3. Add the tomatoes and oregano.
4. Bring to a simmer and cook until the sauce has thickened, about 30 minutes.
5. Season with salt and pepper to taste.
6. Use the sauce immediately or store it in the refrigerator for up to a week.

Garden Journal Prompt:

Reflect on the abundance of your summer garden. Which plants have thrived? What challenges have you faced? What lessons have you learned about gardening in harmony with nature? Record your thoughts and observations in your journal.

August is a month of reflection and anticipation, a time to savour the fruits of our labour while preparing for the transition to autumn. By embracing seed saving and other sustainable gardening practices, we can ensure the continued health and vitality of our gardens, preserving our garden heritage for generations to come.

Chapter 9: Autumn Abundance (September)

September ushers in a season of mellow fruitfulness, a time of rich harvests and vibrant hues. The garden, though beginning its slow retreat into dormancy, is still a haven of life, a testament to the resilience and diversity we've nurtured throughout the year. It's a time to celebrate the abundance of autumn, to savour the flavours of pumpkins, squashes, and apples, and to prepare the garden for its winter slumber. But even as we gather the last of summer's bounty, we must also look ahead, sowing the seeds for future harvests and ensuring the continued health and vitality of our garden ecosystem.

This is a time to reflect on the interconnectedness of all living things, to appreciate the cyclical nature of life and death, and to recognise our role as stewards of the soil, nurturing the very foundation of life in our gardens.

Composting: Nature's Recycling System
Composting is an essential practice for any gardener who embraces the principles of sustainability and biodiversity. It's a way of mimicking nature's own recycling system, transforming garden waste and kitchen scraps into a valuable resource that enriches the soil, feeds our plants, and supports a thriving ecosystem.

It's a simple yet profound act that connects us to the natural cycles of life and death, reminding us that nothing is truly wasted in nature. By composting, we participate in the continuous renewal of life, returning organic matter to the soil from which it came.

- **Understanding the benefits of composting:** Composting offers a multitude of benefits for the garden and the environment. It reduces waste, diverting organic materials from landfills where they would decompose anaerobically and produce harmful greenhouse gases. It creates a nutrient-rich soil amendment that improves soil structure, aeration, and water retention. It supports a thriving ecosystem of beneficial microbes, fungi, and other organisms that contribute to soil health and plant growth. And it reduces the need for synthetic fertilizers, which can harm the environment and disrupt the delicate balance of the soil ecosystem. In essence, composting is a way of closing the loop, returning valuable nutrients to the soil and reducing our reliance on external inputs

- **Building a compost bin or pile:** There are many ways to compost, from simple open piles to more elaborate composting systems. Choose a method that suits your space, budget, and composting needs. A basic compost bin can be constructed from recycled materials, such as pallets or old fence panels. Or you can purchase a ready-made compost bin from a garden centre. The key is to create a contained space where organic materials can decompose in a controlled environment. Consider the aesthetics of your compost bin or pile, integrating it into the overall design of your garden. A well-designed compost area can be both functional and visually appealing.

- **The Art of Composting:** Composting is not just about throwing garden waste into a bin; it's about understanding the process of decomposition and creating the optimal conditions for it to occur. A good compost pile needs a balance of "green" materials, such as grass clippings and kitchen scraps, which are rich in nitrogen, and "brown" materials, such as dried leaves and shredded paper, which are rich in carbon. It also needs adequate moisture and aeration. Turning the compost pile regularly helps to introduce oxygen and speed up the decomposition process. Think of your compost pile as a living organism, requiring the right balance of nutrients, air, and water to thrive.

- **Composting different types of garden waste:** A wide variety of garden waste can be composted, including leaves, grass clippings, plant stems, vegetable scraps, fruit peels, and coffee grounds. Avoid composting diseased plants, meat scraps, or dairy products, as these can attract pests or create unpleasant odours. Shred or chop larger materials to speed up decomposition. And maintain a good balance of green and brown materials to ensure optimal composting conditions. You can also add other organic materials to your compost, such as eggshells, wood ash, and seaweed, to provide additional nutrients and minerals.

- **Troubleshooting your compost:** Even the most experienced composters encounter challenges from time to time. If your compost pile is too wet, add more brown materials or turn it more frequently to improve aeration. If it's too dry, add water or green materials. If it's not decomposing, it may need more nitrogen, so add more green materials or a nitrogen-rich activator, such as comfrey leaves or manure. If you notice unpleasant odours, turn the pile more frequently to improve aeration and reduce anaerobic decomposition.

- **Composting with Worms:** Worm composting, also known as vermicomposting, is a method of composting using worms to break down organic matter. Worms, such as red wigglers, consume organic waste and produce nutrient-rich castings, which are an excellent soil amendment. Worm composting is ideal for smaller spaces and can be done indoors or outdoors. It's a fascinating process to observe, and the resulting castings are a valuable addition to any garden.

September Gardening Tasks
September is a month of transition, a time to harvest the last of summer's bounty while preparing the garden for the cooler days of autumn.

- **Planting fall crops:** There's still time to plant some fall crops, such as lettuce, spinach, kale, and radishes. These cool-season crops can tolerate light frosts and provide fresh produce well into the autumn. Prepare the soil by removing weeds and adding compost. Sow seeds or transplant seedlings according to the specific needs of each crop. Consider using row covers or cloches to protect young plants from early frosts and extend the growing season.

- **Cleaning up the garden:** As summer crops fade, remove spent plants and weeds to prevent the spread of pests and diseases. Compost healthy plant debris to recycle nutrients and reduce waste. If you suspect any diseased plants, dispose of them carefully to avoid contaminating other areas of the garden. You can also chop and drop spent crops, leaving them on the soil surface to decompose and add organic matter. This provides a natural mulch that helps to suppress weeds and protect the soil.

- **Protecting plants from early frosts:** Early frosts can damage or kill tender plants. Protect vulnerable plants with cloches, row covers, or cold frames. Bring potted plants indoors or move them to a sheltered location. And consider mulching around plants to insulate the soil and protect roots from frost damage. You can also use horticultural fleece to protect plants from frost. This lightweight material allows light and air to pass through while providing insulation.

Featured Plant: Pumpkin (Cucurbita pepo)
Pumpkins are iconic symbols of autumn, their vibrant orange hues and versatile uses adding a touch of warmth and cheer to the season. But pumpkins are more than just decorative gourds. Their nectar-rich flowers attract pollinators, providing a late-season food source for bees and butterflies. Their seeds provide a nutritious snack for birds and other wildlife. And their flesh can be used to create a variety of culinary delights, from savoury soups and stews to sweet pies and breads.

Pumpkins are relatively easy to grow, thriving in full sun and fertile, well-drained soil. They require plenty of space to spread their vines and benefit from regular watering, especially during dry periods.

The Wonderful World of Pumpkins
Pumpkins belong to the Cucurbitaceae family, which also includes squash, melons, and cucumbers. They are native to North America and have been cultivated for thousands of years. Pumpkins are a rich source of vitamins, minerals, and antioxidants. They are also a good source of fibre, which can help with digestion and weight management.

Pumpkins are not only delicious but also versatile. They can be used in a variety of dishes, from savoury soups and stews to sweet pies and breads. Their seeds can be roasted and eaten as a snack or used to make pumpkin seed oil. And their flesh can be used to create a variety of decorative items, such as jack-o'-lanterns and Thanksgiving centrepieces.

DIY Project: Creating a Scarecrow
Creating a scarecrow is a fun and traditional way to add a touch of whimsy to the autumn garden while deterring birds from feasting on your ripening crops. Use recycled materials, such as old clothes, straw, and sticks, to create a unique and charming scarecrow that will stand guard over your garden.

Garden Journal Prompt:
Reflect on the changing seasons in your garden. How has the garden transformed from the vibrant days of summer to the mellow hues of autumn? What lessons have you learned from the gardening year? What are your hopes and plans for the coming seasons? Record your thoughts and observations in your journal.

September is a month of gratitude and reflection, a time to appreciate the abundance of the garden and prepare for the coming winter. By embracing composting and other sustainable gardening practices, we can ensure the continued health and vitality of our gardens, creating a haven for both plants and wildlife throughout the changing seasons.

Chapter 10: Preparing for Winter (October)

October arrives, a month of swirling leaves, crisp air, and the final flourish of autumn's palette. The garden, though surrendering to the embrace of dormancy, still hums with a quiet vitality, a testament to the enduring strength of the ecosystem we've nurtured. It's a time to gather the last of the harvest, to savour the lingering warmth of the sun, and to prepare the garden for its winter slumber. But even as we bid farewell to the vibrant growth of summer, we must also remember that life persists, albeit in a more subtle form. This is a time to shift our focus from abundance to preservation, ensuring that the garden remains a haven for life, even in the depths of winter.

Protecting Beneficial Insects Over Winter: A Sanctuary for Small Lives

As temperatures drop and the days grow shorter, our thoughts turn to protecting the beneficial insects that have played such a vital role in the garden's success throughout the year. These tiny creatures, our silent partners in pollination, pest control, and soil health, deserve our care and consideration as they seek shelter from the approaching cold. By providing them with safe havens, we ensure their survival and contribute to the continued health and vitality of our garden ecosystem.

Resist the urge to tidy up too meticulously in autumn. Leaf litter, hollow stems, and clumps of grasses provide vital refuge for overwintering insects. These natural shelters offer protection from the elements and provide a source of food and insulation. Create designated areas in your garden where you leave leaves and plant debris undisturbed, allowing insects to find shelter and complete their life cycles. Consider creating a "wildlife zone" in a quiet corner of your garden where you allow nature to take its course, providing a haven for insects, amphibians, and other creatures.

Many pollinators, such as bumblebees and solitary bees, overwinter in the ground or in hollow stems. Leave some areas of bare ground undisturbed for ground-nesting bees. Bundle together hollow stems, such as bamboo canes or sunflower stalks, and place them in a sheltered location to provide nesting sites for solitary bees. You can also create, or purchase bee houses specifically designed for overwintering pollinators. Place these bee houses in a sunny, sheltered location, facing south or east to catch the morning sun.

Deadwood, often considered an eyesore in tidy gardens, plays a vital role in supporting biodiversity. Standing dead trees, fallen logs, and decaying branches provide habitat for a wide range of insects, fungi, and other organisms. These organisms contribute to the decomposition process, recycling nutrients and enriching the soil. They also provide food and shelter for birds, bats, and other wildlife. Consider leaving some deadwood in your garden, creating a natural haven for these vital creatures. If you have space, create a "dead hedge" by piling branches and twigs between stakes. This provides valuable habitat for insects and small mammals.

While some tidying up is necessary in autumn, avoid excessive cleaning that can disrupt insect habitats. Leave some leaves on the ground to provide shelter for insects and other organisms. Delay cutting back perennials until spring, as their hollow stems can provide overwintering sites for beneficial insects. Also, avoid disturbing areas where insects may be overwintering, such as compost heaps, log piles, and leaf litter. Remember that a tidy garden is not necessarily a biodiverse garden. Embrace the natural beauty of decay and allow nature to take its course.

Creating Winter Interest in the Garden
While the garden may be winding down for the year, we can still create visual interest and provide for wildlife during the winter months.

Consider planting late-blooming flowers, such as asters, goldenrod, and sedums, to provide a late-season nectar source for pollinators. Include plants with colourful berries, such as holly, cotoneaster, and pyracantha, to provide food for birds and add visual interest to the winter landscape.

Plant evergreen shrubs and trees to provide structure and shelter for wildlife. And consider adding decorative elements, such as bird feeders, bird baths, and sculptures, to enhance the beauty of the winter garden.

October Gardening Tasks

October is a month of transition, a time to harvest the last of the summer's bounty while preparing the garden for the colder months ahead.

- **Harvesting late-season crops:** Gather the last of your summer crops, such as tomatoes, peppers, squash, and root vegetables. Store them properly for winter use. Consider preserving any surplus by canning, freezing, or drying.

- **Planting cover crops:** Cover crops, such as clover, rye, or vetch, are sown in autumn to protect and improve the soil over winter. They help to prevent soil erosion, suppress weeds, and add nutrients to the soil as they decompose. Choose cover crops that are suited to your climate and soil conditions.

- **Mulching garden beds:** Apply a layer of mulch, such as compost, shredded leaves, or bark chips, to your garden beds to insulate the soil, protect plant roots from frost damage, and suppress weeds. Mulch also helps to retain moisture and improve soil health as it decomposes.

- **Preparing your pond for winter:** If you have a pond, take steps to prepare it for winter. Remove any fallen leaves and debris that could decompose and pollute the water. Reduce the amount of food you give to fish, as their metabolism slows down in colder temperatures. And consider installing a pond heater or aerator to prevent the pond from freezing solid, which can harm fish and other aquatic life.

Featured Plant: Aster (Aster spp.)
Asters are a welcome sight in the autumn garden, their cheerful blooms adding a splash of colour to the fading landscape. These hardy perennials are also valuable contributors to the biodiversity of the garden, providing a late-season nectar source for pollinators, such as bees, butterflies, and hoverflies. Asters come in a variety of colours, from vibrant purples and pinks to delicate blues and whites. They are relatively low-maintenance and thrive in full sun or partial shade. Plant them in borders, meadows, or wildflower gardens to attract pollinators and extend the season of bloom.

The Importance of Late-Season Nectar Sources
As the days grow shorter and temperatures drop, pollinators need all the help they can get to prepare for winter. Late-blooming plants, such as asters, goldenrod, and sedums, provide a crucial source of nectar and pollen, helping pollinators build up their energy reserves for the winter months. By including these plants in our gardens, we can support the health and survival of these vital creatures.

DIY Project: Building a hibernaculum
This is a shelter designed to provide a safe and cozy overwintering spot for beneficial insects, amphibians, and even reptiles.
(Include detailed instructions for building a hibernaculum using natural materials, such as logs, branches, leaves, and stones. Explain how to create different compartments within the hibernaculum to cater to the needs of different creatures.)

Garden Journal Prompt:
Reflect on the changing seasons in your garden. How has the garden transformed from the vibrant days of summer to the quieter days of autumn? What steps have you taken to protect wildlife and prepare the garden for winter? Record your thoughts and observations in your journal.

October is a month of preparation and reflection, a time to appreciate the abundance of the past season and prepare for the challenges and opportunities of the coming winter. By embracing sustainable gardening practices and providing for the needs of wildlife, we can ensure that our gardens remain havens of life throughout the changing seasons.

Chapter 11: Winter Rest (November)

November descends, casting a veil of tranquillity over the garden. The once vibrant tapestry of life has faded to muted hues, the air is crisp and still, and the earth rests beneath a blanket of fallen leaves. It's a time of introspection, a moment to pause and reflect on the journey we've taken through the seasons, to acknowledge the successes and challenges we've encountered, and to prepare ourselves and our gardens for the quietude of winter.

While the outward signs of life may be diminishing, the garden remains a sanctuary, a place of quiet beauty and enduring resilience. This is a time to appreciate the subtle nuances of the season, to find beauty in the starkness of the landscape, and to recognise the importance of rest and renewal in the cycle of life.

Reflecting on the Season: A Time for Introspection

As the gardening year draws to a close, it's a valuable practice to take stock of our experiences, to learn from our successes and failures, and to plan for the seasons ahead. This is a time to delve into our garden journals, to revisit the observations and reflections we've recorded throughout the year, and to glean insights that will guide our future gardening endeavours. It's a moment to acknowledge the interconnectedness of all living things, to recognise our role as stewards of the earth, and to deepen our understanding of the natural world.

Recall the highlights of the gardening year. Which plants thrived? What new techniques did you try? What were your proudest achievements? Perhaps you successfully grew a new variety of tomato, or perhaps you created a thriving habitat for pollinators.

Equally important, reflect on the challenges you faced. Which plants struggled? Were there any pest or disease outbreaks? What lessons can you learn from these experiences? By honestly assessing our successes and failures, we gain valuable knowledge that will inform our future gardening decisions. We learn to adapt our practices, to experiment with new approaches, and to embrace the unpredictable nature of gardening.

November is an ideal time to start planning for the next growing season. Review your garden journal, noting which plants performed well and which ones struggled. Consider what new varieties you want to try, and research their specific needs and growing requirements. Sketch out a plan for your garden beds, considering crop rotation, companion planting, and the needs of different plants. Order seeds and supplies early to ensure you have everything you need for a successful start to the season. This is also a good time to assess your tools and equipment, making any necessary repairs or replacements.

A garden journal is an invaluable tool for any gardener, a record of our experiences, observations, and reflections. It's a place to document the successes and challenges we encounter, to track the growth and development of our plants, and to capture the fleeting beauty of the garden throughout the seasons. A garden journal can be as simple or as elaborate as you like. It can be a notebook filled with handwritten notes and sketches, or a digital document with photos and detailed records. The key is to make it your own, a personal reflection of your gardening journey. Use your journal to record not only the practical aspects of gardening but also your emotional responses to the garden, the sights, sounds, and smells that evoke a sense of wonder and connection with the natural world.

The Garden in Winter: A Time of Dormancy and Renewal
While the garden may appear dormant in winter, life persists beneath the surface. Plants are storing energy, roots are growing, and insects are overwintering in sheltered nooks and crannies. Winter is a time of rest and renewal, a period of preparation for the burst of growth that will come with spring.

It's a time to appreciate the subtle beauty of the season, the stark silhouettes of bare branches against the winter sky, the frost-covered leaves sparkling in the morning sun, and the quietude that pervades the landscape.

Embracing the Winter Garden
Even in winter, the garden offers opportunities for connection and enjoyment. Take a walk through the garden and observe the subtle signs of life. Listen to the birdsong, watch the squirrels scampering through the trees, and admire the winter-flowering plants that brave the cold.

Create winter interest by planting evergreens, such as holly, yew, and conifers, which provide structure and colour to the winter landscape. Add decorative elements, such as bird feeders, bird baths, and sculptures, to enhance the beauty of the winter garden. And consider creating a winter garden specifically designed to provide food and shelter for wildlife during the colder months.

November Gardening Tasks
Although the garden is winding down for the year, there are still a few essential tasks to attend to in November.

- **Protecting tender plants from frost:** As temperatures drop, protect tender plants from frost damage. Bring potted plants indoors or move them to a sheltered location. Cover vulnerable plants with cloches, row covers, or horticultural fleece. And mulch around plants to insulate the soil and protect roots from frost.

- **Cleaning and storing garden tools:** Clean and sharpen your garden tools before storing them for the winter. This will prevent rust and ensure that your tools are in good condition for the next growing season. Store tools in a dry and sheltered location to protect them from the elements.

- **Ordering seeds and supplies for next year:** November is a good time to order seeds and supplies for the next growing season. Many seed companies offer early bird discounts and have a wider selection of varieties available at this time of year. Ordering early ensures that you have everything you need for a successful start to the season.

- **Winter pruning:** Some plants benefit from winter pruning, while they are dormant. This is a good time to prune deciduous shrubs, such as roses and fruit trees, to remove dead or diseased wood and shape the plants for the next growing season. Avoid pruning spring-flowering shrubs, as this can remove flower buds.

- **Preparing for winter wildlife:** Continue to provide food and shelter for wildlife during the winter months. Keep bird feeders stocked with seeds and suet. Provide fresh water in bird baths. And leave areas of leaf litter and plant debris undisturbed to provide shelter for insects and other creatures.

Featured Plant: Holly (Ilex spp.)
Holly is a symbol of winter cheer, its glossy evergreen leaves and vibrant red berries adding a touch of festive colour to the garden. But holly is more than just a decorative plant. It provides vital food and shelter for wildlife during the winter months.

Its dense foliage offers protection from the elements, and its berries provide a valuable food source for birds, especially when other food sources are scarce. Holly is a dioecious plant, meaning that male and female flowers are borne on separate plants. To ensure berry production, plant both male and female holly plants.

The Holly and the Ivy: A Winter Tradition

Holly and ivy have long been associated with winter celebrations and traditions. In pre-Christian times, holly was considered a symbol of life and rebirth, while ivy was associated with immortality and eternity. These plants were often used to decorate homes and churches during the winter solstice, symbolising the triumph of light over darkness. Today, holly and ivy remain popular Christmas decorations, reminding us of the enduring spirit of life and hope during the darkest days of the year.

Creative Project: Making Holiday Decorations with Natural Materials

Embrace the spirit of the season by creating festive decorations using natural materials from your garden. Gather pinecones, holly branches, berries, and seed pods to create wreaths, garlands, and other festive adornments. These natural decorations add a touch of rustic charm to your home and celebrate the beauty of the natural world.

Garden Journal Prompt:

Reflect on the past gardening year. What were your greatest successes and challenges? What lessons have you learned? What are your hopes and plans for the next growing season? Record your thoughts and observations in your journal. November is a month of quietude and reflection, a time to appreciate the beauty of the fading season and prepare for the stillness of winter. By taking stock of our experiences, planning, and providing for the needs of wildlife, we can ensure that our gardens remain havens of life throughout the changing seasons.

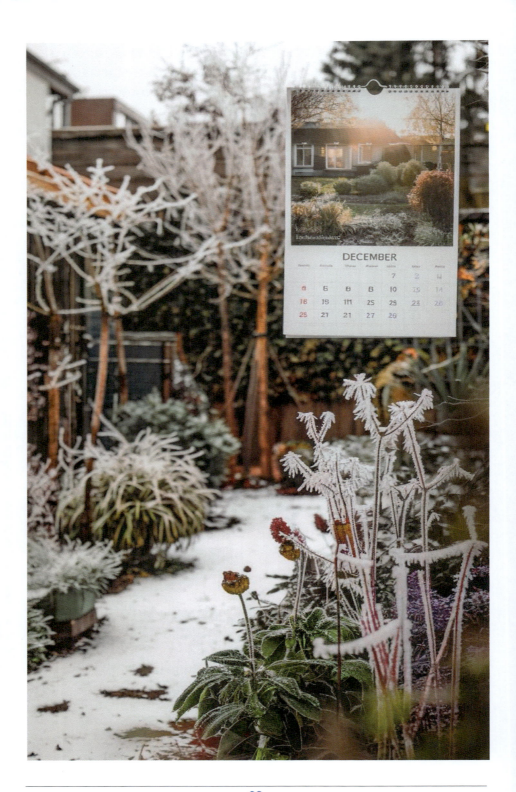

Chapter 12: A Time for Renewal (December)

December arrives, cloaked in the stillness of winter. The garden slumbers, its vibrant tapestry of life now a tapestry of muted hues, frosted leaves, and skeletal branches reaching towards the pale sky. It's a time of quietude, a moment to embrace the cyclical nature of the garden, to acknowledge the necessity of rest and retreat, and to anticipate the promise of renewal that lies dormant within the earth.

While the outward show of life may have dwindled, the garden remains a sanctuary, a place of subtle beauty and enduring resilience. This is a time to connect with the deeper rhythms of nature, to find solace in the stillness, and to nurture our own connection to the earth, recognising that we too are part of this intricate web of life, subject to the ebb and flow of the seasons.

The Importance of Rest: Allowing Nature to Take its Course
Just as we need periods of rest and rejuvenation, so too does the garden. Winter is a time for the soil to replenish itself, for organisms to retreat into dormancy, and for the natural cycles of decomposition to enrich the earth. It's a time to let go of the active tending and embrace the quieter rhythms of the season, allowing nature to weave its magic of restoration and renewal.

Resist the urge to over-manage the garden in winter. Leave some areas undisturbed, allowing leaf litter and plant debris to provide shelter for overwintering insects and other creatures. Avoid excessive digging or tilling, which can disrupt the soil structure and harm beneficial organisms. Allow the soil to rest and regenerate, building its fertility and resilience for the seasons ahead. This is a time to trust in the wisdom of nature, to recognise that the garden has its own inherent rhythm and that by stepping back, we allow it to follow its natural course.

Winter is not a time of inactivity in the garden; it's a time of unseen activity, a period of subtle transformations and preparations for the future. Beneath the surface, roots are growing, microbes are decomposing organic matter, and seeds are lying dormant, awaiting the warmth of spring to awaken. By observing the garden in winter, we can gain a deeper understanding of these hidden processes and appreciate the cyclical nature of life. We can learn to recognise the signs of life that persist even in the depths of winter, the subtle movements of creatures seeking shelter, the swelling buds on branches, and the promise of new life held within the dormant seeds.

While the garden rests, we can engage in the enjoyable task of planning for the year ahead. Review your garden journal, noting the successes and challenges of the past year. Dream of new possibilities, research new plant varieties, and sketch out plans for your garden beds. Order seeds and supplies, anticipating the joy of sowing and planting in the coming months. Winter is a time for reflection and anticipation, a time to nurture our gardening dreams and prepare for the season of renewal. It's a time to explore new ideas, to experiment with different approaches, and to expand our gardening horizons.

Even in the depths of winter, the garden offers opportunities for connection and enjoyment. Bundle up and take a walk through the garden, observing the subtle beauty of frost-covered leaves, the intricate patterns of bare branches, and the winter-flowering plants that brave the cold. Listen to the birdsong, watch the squirrels scampering through the trees, and breathe in the crisp winter air. These moments of connection with nature nourish our souls and remind us of the enduring beauty and resilience of the natural world. They offer a sense of peace and tranquillity, a respite from the hustle and bustle of daily life.

The Winter Solstice: A Time of Rebirth

The winter solstice, the shortest day of the year, marks a turning point in the cycle of the seasons. It's a time of rebirth, a moment to celebrate the return of the light and the promise of new beginnings. In many cultures, the winter solstice is celebrated with rituals and traditions that honour the cyclical nature of life and the enduring power of nature. Consider incorporating some of these traditions into your own winter celebrations, creating a meaningful connection to the season and the natural world.

December Gardening Tasks

December may be a quiet month in the garden, but there are still a few tasks to attend to, ensuring that the garden remains a haven for life throughout the winter.

- **Winter pruning of deciduous trees:** December is a good time to prune deciduous trees, while they are dormant. Remove any dead, diseased, or crossing branches to maintain the health and shape of the trees. This is also a good time to remove any branches that may pose a hazard during winter storms.

- **Forcing bulbs for indoor blooms:** Bring a touch of spring indoors by forcing bulbs, such as hyacinths, daffodils, and tulips. Plant the bulbs in pots with potting mix and place them in a cool, dark location for several weeks to encourage root development. Once the roots have developed, bring the pots into a warmer, brighter location to encourage flowering. This is a delightful way to enjoy the beauty of flowers during the winter months and to anticipate the arrival of spring.

- **Enjoying the winter garden:** Even in winter, the garden offers a sense of peace and tranquillity. Take time to appreciate the subtle beauty of the season, the stark silhouettes of bare branches against the winter sky, the frost-covered leaves sparkling in the morning sun, and the quietude that pervades the landscape. Create winter interest by planting evergreens, such as holly, yew, and conifers, which provide structure and colour to the winter landscape. Add decorative elements, such as bird feeders, bird baths, and sculptures, to enhance the beauty of the winter garden. And consider creating a winter garden specifically designed to provide food and shelter for wildlife during the colder months.

Featured Plant: Winterberry (Ilex verticillata)
Winterberry is a deciduous holly that adds a splash of vibrant colour to the winter garden. Its bright red berries, which persist after the leaves have fallen, provide a valuable food source for birds and other wildlife during the colder months. Winterberry is a dioecious plant, meaning that male and female flowers are borne on separate plants. To ensure berry production, plant both male and female winterberry plants. Winterberry thrives in moist, acidic soil and full sun or partial shade. It's a relatively low-maintenance plant that adds beauty and ecological value to the winter garden.

The Folklore of Winterberry
Winterberry has a rich folklore and symbolism associated with it. In some cultures, it is believed to represent hope, perseverance, and the enduring spirit of life during the darkest days of winter. Its bright red berries are also associated with good luck and prosperity.

In Native American cultures, winterberry was used for medicinal purposes and was believed to have protective powers. Incorporating winterberry into your garden not only adds beauty and ecological value but also connects you to the rich cultural heritage associated with this plant.

Personal Reflection: The Joys of Gardening for Biodiversity

As we reach the end of our journey through the gardening year, I invite you to reflect on the joys and rewards of gardening for biodiversity. It's a practice that connects us to the natural world, fosters a sense of wonder and appreciation for the intricate web of life, and empowers us to become active participants in the creation of a more sustainable and harmonious world. By embracing the principles of biodiversity, we create gardens that are not only beautiful but also resilient, productive, and teeming with life. We nurture not only our plants but also the soil, the pollinators, the birds, and all the creatures that contribute to the health and vitality of our gardens. And in doing so, we nurture our own connection to the earth and our sense of place in the web of life.

Gardening as a Spiritual Practice

Gardening can be more than just a hobby or a way to produce food; it can also be a spiritual practice that connects us to the deeper rhythms of life and the natural world. The act of tending to the garden, of nurturing life and observing the cycles of growth and decay, can be a source of profound meaning and connection. It can teach us patience, humility, and respect for the interconnectedness of all living things. And it can provide us with a sense of peace and tranquillity, a refuge from the stresses of modern life.

The End... and a New Beginning

As the year draws to a close, we find ourselves at the threshold of a new beginning. The garden rests, awaiting the return of spring, when the cycle of life will begin anew. But even in the depths of winter, the seeds of renewal are present, dormant within the earth, awaiting the warmth of the sun to awaken them. And so, we too can embrace this time of rest and reflection, nurturing our own inner seeds of creativity, hope, and renewal, preparing ourselves for the joys and challenges of the gardening year to come.

Printed in Great Britain
by Amazon